The RIGHT side:
A look at Controversy and Critical Thinking

Copyright Lance Hodge, 2018

ISBN-13: 978-1720475842

Printed in the United States of America

"No way of thinking or doing,
however ancient, can be trusted
without proof." –

Henry David Thoreau

A Critical Thinking Publication
Volume 1

The RIGHT side:

A look at Controversy and Critical Thinking

By Lance Hodge

"Education is what remains after one has forgotten everything one learned in school."

- Albert Einstein

The RIGHT side:

A look at Controversy and Critical Thinking

By Lance Hodge

They say that college students, and young people in general, are *indoctrinated* by their liberal professors, and that they are easily manipulated by media. The vast majority of college professors *are* liberals, and liberals are on a mission to spread liberal thought, so that seems logical. And, young people put way too much emphasis on the "news" they get from *social media* sources, so that seems logical as well. And you young people reading this, *you* know how much effort *you* put into examining both sides of issues in the news, is it significant, or not? Do you trust the source when you hear a controversial story, or distrust it and try to seek out the facts yourself? Most of you probably do very little independent research, and trust that the source is telling the truth, without some political agenda that colors that "truth." The term "fake news" was once bestowed upon the conservative media by liberals, but has now come full circle, with the liberal media the subject of that mantra, and earning it daily. Could it be that the liberal media has fully embraced one political party, and is indeed *shaping* the "news" in favor of their political views? The answer to that rhetorical question is *yes*. Journalism is thought to be independent, in search of the truth, careful not to insert personal opinion into the reporting of *news*, but, "journalism" has largely abandoned that charge, choosing instead to become an *advocate* of liberalism, and freely bending the truth, and even ignoring certain facts, in favor of service to a political agenda. The liberal media is now a willing tool of that liberal agenda. THAT is a big deal, that is a game-changer. Without an independent and fair media, we lose our primary guardian against tyranny, and worse yet, when that media becomes an arm of one political party, we open the door wide to such tyranny.

This liberal indoctrination/*brainwashing* is present in the majority of social media, the *news*, in Hollywood movies and television shows, comedy, etc., in just about every aspect of life young people will face a constant onslaught of the *liberal* view of things. The liberal viewpoint is the predominant viewpoint in schools, and in most "mainstream" media. *Political correctness* is running rampant, and a different point of view is quickly labeled "hate." People are shouted down, threatened with violence and called "racists," for daring to have an opposing view.

In this book I'll attempt to undo some of that, or to at least offer up that *other* view, the one you might not hear without a liberal spin on it. I won't try to thoroughly argue my points here, the pros and cons and alternate positions on all these issues would fill a phone book, and *this* book is by design going to be short. But I won't lie, what I say in this book isn't just my opinion, it's based on well-established *fact*. Even the above review of the state of journalism, and the arrival of a clearly biased liberal media, this is not speculation, this **is** the current state of our "news."

One thing to realize, which is most likely the *key* to understanding the liberal mind, is that liberal thought may be the result of *defective thinking*. If you're a liberal, and you're already getting mad, good, I'm making a point, and *emotion* is part of this point. Although it may be difficult for young people to accept, or to admit this, the fact is that our brains don't mature until about age **twenty-five**. This fact explains so much, it answers the question "Why are so many liberals ignoring clear *facts* in favor of *emotion* when it comes to controversial topics?"

The prefrontal cortex is responsible for long-term planning, the ability to apply logic and common sense to the issues we confront, and to use *critical thinking* skills to evaluate alternate views of an issue. Until our brains have matured we are susceptible to that indoctrination I spoke of, and we are *prone* to it. The ability to think *critically*, and to seek out facts to prove or disprove notions presented to us, is vital to the development of a fully capable prefrontal cortex. If we do not *consistently* use those neuro connections to develop these critical thinking skills during those formative years, those unused pathways are ultimately *pruned away* during brain development, and we may have impeded the *ability* of our brains to *do* such thinking in the future, we may indeed suffer *damage* to our brains, that might be permanent, if during the brain's development we simply go along with the crowd and not think for ourselves. That is the danger of such liberal indoctrination before age twenty-five. Liberals know how susceptible our youth are, and they exploit it. During these formative years we must not simply accept as fact what comes to us from our professors, our social or other media, or our peers, we must seek out unbiased facts, and decide for ourselves.

The world, well, at least the United States, is essentially divided in half as far as political views; there are *liberals*, and *conservatives*. A relative small portion of us usually turn the election one way or the other, usually based on some particular wedge issue which hits a personal nerve at election time, giving one or the other party the advantage in any particular election cycle, which is one reason why we alternate regularly between democrats or conservatives in charge.

Most liberals are *democrats* and most conservatives are *republicans*. Believing in conservative values is the majority view, more people identify as conservative than liberal, but you'd think the opposite, listening to the "news." There are other parties, but they don't win elections, not yet. These *other* parties are often the great mass of "undecided" that they speak of and try to convince to join one side or the other during each election cycle. Generally, the liberal will not vote for a conservative, and the conservative will not vote for a liberal, those groups generally stick with their respective side, and so those undecideds become a key factor. Being *undecided*, and able to vote conservative in one election and liberal in the next, is also a sign of someone with a loose political or moral compass, basically they are empty vessels waiting to swing this way or that depending on who puts out the most convincing propaganda. I know, you might think this is an *opinion* of mine and not a fact, but, it's a *fact*.

Liberals are considered to the *left* of center, and republicans to the *right* of center. If you're **far-left** you're probably a socialist or something close to it, and if you're *far-right* you're, well, liberals might say far-right is skin-head Nazis or members of the KKK, but far-right is more reasonably the *Tea Party* types; if we're going to call republicans *right*, the Tea Party is further right than them. To liberals The Tea Party **is** far-right, equivalent to those Nazis and skinheads. The Tea Party isn't an actual *party*, it's a mind-set, one that doesn't identify much with your old-school republicans, and are often loathe to identify themselves as one of them. The Tea Party, or those further right than republicans, want to return to stricter *constitutional* principles as spelled out in our Constitution, like a small federal government with very limited scope and power, with most powers reserved for the states, limited taxation, and limited intrusion into our lives by that constitutionally limited federal government. The Tea Party has been grossly mischaracterized by the left into some far-right caricature, when it is quite simply a movement to return to the strict constitutional principles that our founders outlined in that old dusty parchment called *The Constitution.*

 The liberal mantra goes something like this; conservatives (we'll just call them Republicans) hate the planet, love dirty air and water, and look forward, for some reason, to the hideous planetary destruction from global warming that is right around the corner. They LOVE guns, more than kids, more than anything except the Bible. They are obsessively devoted to God and all manner of illogical ancient beliefs in The Bible (although this one comes and goes, from time to time liberals will embrace God and the Bible for political reasons) and republicans are Capitalists, which means they are greedy, and they only care about money, to hell with helping the homeless or helping people with welfare or food stamps, they're heartless bastards. And, they're racists, of course republicans are all about WHITE, and hate every other color or shade, especially brown and black. Republicans like civil war statues that remind them of the South, and they wish we could make black people slaves again, they LOVED slavery. Republicans want to control women's bodies, not allowing them to have abortions. Oil, republicans are all about oil, drilling for oil, destroying the earth for oil, polluting our air and water with oil, and profiting from oil, they love BIG OIL and big corporations. It's all about profit. They HATE wind power or solar power, and *love* power sources that ruin the planet. Republicans are backward rednecks and ignorant uneducated haters unable to see that the world has changed and is changing even more, leaving them and their ancient ways behind. Conservatism is old and backward, liberals are "progressive" and forward thinking. Oh, and the conservative hate for brown people, well that's clear, republicans are *obsessed* with borders, and keeping people who want to come to the U.S. out, *especially* those hated Mexicans. I almost forgot Muslims, republicans HATE Muslims, all Muslims, republicans don't understand that we are all the same, we are one people, one race, the human race, and Muslims are just like any other religion in that regard, Islam is the "religion of peace." There's more, but that's a good start. I'll date this book by mentioning Donald Trump, although he'll most likely be the President until 2024 so I've got a few years before I need to update this; and you *know* republicans are **crazy**, and wrong about everything, that's just obvious, it's crystal clear, because *they* voted for Donald Trump!

If the preceding rant on the liberal mindset seemed pretty accurate to you, well, that liberal indoctrination I spoke of has worked. Let me go though that list of beliefs again…

Conservatives, using critical thinking, and *facts*, don't buy into the whole **global warming** mantra. The science is NOT clear, as a matter of fact, the planet had a decade long cooling period that doesn't fit the global CO2 warming narrative at all, and now, we're currently in a two-year cooling trend, with some scientists thinking we may actually be in for *global **cooling***. You know of the stories that revealed many scientists falsified temperature data to support their global warming theory? That the scientific community is NOT of one mind when it comes to man-made global warming, right? Your trusted media told you about that, right?

Of course republicans *love* not hate the planet, they live here too, and they prefer clean air and water, but don't want to shut down our economic growth with over-the-top controls and regulations that do more to hurt the economy than to protect the planet. A few years ago, the liberal protest of a pipeline was a big deal. A pipeline is a *good* thing, oil is a good thing, our economy depends on oil, and a pipeline is more cost effective and safer than ground transportation and can be built with environmental safety as a top concern, and pipeline spills are quite rare, and cause minimal short-lived impact when they do happen.

As far as **guns**, republicans realize our country's constitution has enshrined the right to own guns for self-defense, and as a means to protect ourselves from an oppressive or tyrannical government. You might recall how America was founded, it was a revolution, with guns, and without guns we would have had no recourse against oppressive British control and domination.

Republicans do tend to identify as "**religious**" more than liberals, but biblical principles are generally aligned with long-standing societal norms, which tend to be norms for a reason, they tend to preserve order and reinforce long-accepted standards. There is some potential harm to a society when *anything goes*, and when norms are thrown out the window in favor of the popular trends of the day. Allowing anyone to marry anyone or anything tends to lessen what marriage is, and such trendy redefinitions are not always in the best interest of a healthy society long-term. The one man one woman definition of marriage was supported by Hillary Clinton *and* Barack Obama, until it became more politically helpful to change that opinion. You knew that about them, didn't you?

Republicans are proudly **Capitalists**. Capitalism is the economic engine that has made our country the financial powerhouse of the world and the envy of most other nations. Capitalism has allowed us to prosper so greatly that we give more than any other nation on earth to others around the world. The United States is a generous and *good* nation, helping people and trying to advocate for freedom from oppression around the world.

Republicans are more likely to try to limit things like welfare and food stamps, after proving that long-term handouts tend to create a permanent underclass that is *dependent* on such welfare. Republicans are more likely to push for a temporary helping hand while encouraging the poor to move up and out of poverty, through job training and education intent on allowing those people to enter the workforce and become self-sufficient. By a large margin, republicans are much more giving and generous than liberals, their voluntary contributions to help people in need far outpace liberals. If that's a surprise to you, someone's been editing your news.

Racists? The republican party is the party of Lincoln and emancipation. Southern *democrats* were the party of the KKK and consistently fought the republicans as they worked for civil rights and racial equality. During the Clinton years there was a democratic former KKK member on the senate, (Robert Byrd, served from 1959-2010) and he was loved and admired by Bill Clinton and the democratic establishment. Hillary Clinton called Robert Byrd her "friend and mentor." *Republican* racism just doesn't stand up to even a little scrutiny.

That old dusty constitution began the long road to equality and freedom, by proclaiming it as a standard, and knowing it was no easy or quick task in the world of the 1700's to fully realize it, but knowing it would eventually come. Our Constitution and our founding was all about a new equality of man, and those most opposed to it were democrats in the south.

The Governor of Alabama, fighting in the 60's to keep blacks and whites segregated, was a democrat. That list goes on and on, turning on its head the notion that republicans are the party of racists and racism, when quite the opposite is true.

That indoctrination I spoke of works. That *racist* Tea Party I mentioned earlier embraced many black political candidates and members, even a black republican Presidential candidate.

Republicans think **abortion** is the murder of an unborn child, because, *abortion is the murder of an unborn child*. Liberals try to call such children something else, but they're *children*. If a liberal woman was shot in the belly and her baby was killed, the killer would be charged with murder, because "it" isn't a "thing" it's a *child*. If you think abortions should be easy and plentiful, you should probably try plugging in some of that critical thinking I've been talking about. It seems logical that we should be trying to *prevent* the killing of unborn babies, not embracing it, not normalizing it, and not applauding it, right? Are you feeling brainwashed yet? You have been, they've worked hard to make you push aside common sense in favor of some *movement*. Now where's my pink hat.

Oil. Republicans *are* in favor of oil, drilling for oil, getting more oil, having cheaper and plentiful oil. We rely on oil. Solar and wind power, even if *hugely* expanded *can't replace oil*. Some magic new power source will probably be discovered, but we don't have that yet. So we need to use oil, do it as safely as possible, and make its use as clean as is reasonably possible. Massive cuts to oil production or increased taxation or costs upon the oil industry will make gas more expensive and could cripple our economy. Liberals used to be quite opposed to nuclear power, considering the devastating consequences of a large nuclear accident, but now they seem to embrace it. Republicans too seem to be OK with nuclear power. Using dangerous nuclear isotopes to boil water to make steam to turn turbines to generate electricity is NOT smart. It's tremendously expensive, the expensive nuclear power plants only last a few decades, their wastes need to be "safely" stored, someplace, for *thousands* of years, and when the nuclear power plant is decommissioned they remain a deadly toxic risk to us and the environment for *thousands* of years! Not smart. So we're stuck with oil, until some new cleaner source can replace it.

  The technology for wind power or solar power cannot replace our need for oil, it can't even come close. Did you know that wind power kills thousands and thousands of birds of prey? Eagles, hawks, falcons, even endangered species. Thousands and thousands killed by rotating windmills. And solar power, *free* power from the sun, requires massive pollution to *make* those solar panels, and requires dangerous and highly polluting lead batteries to hold that power. Most electric cars, when plugged in to recharge, are recharging with power from a coal-fired power plant, not solar or wind power. You knew that right? If we *all* had solar cars, the vast majority of that electrical power would be coming from a conventional powerplant, not solar or wind. You knew that? We could cover the country with solar panels and windmills and still need oil as our primary energy source.

  Yes, republicans *are* obsessed with **borders** and keeping people who want to come to the U.S. illegally, out. Because you MUST have borders to have a country. Especially with a country like the U.S. who gives massive amounts of welfare and taxpayer funded free stuff to anyone who arrives. We simply can't afford to feed, educate, house, and take care of the health problems of anyone and everyone who shows up. Yes, we need a strong border, yes, we need a border wall, duh.

Muslims. Muslims are not the same as *us* (Meaning non-Muslims.) Have you paid attention to what goes on in majority Muslim countries around the world? The treatment of those of different religions, LGBTQ's, women; you've noticed, I hope, that they have a VERY different view when it comes to personal freedom. Islam allows, actually mandates, some pretty terrible behavior. Do I need to list it? I hope not, you pay attention to events around the world when deciding what and who you believe, right? We should be careful about letting Muslims into our country that hate us and seek to replace, by force, all the world's other religions with Islam. "Death to America" is a common Muslim chant, and they mean it. A little research into Islam will show that it is a quite different religion, one that seeks domination, by force. That's NOT the same as the other world religions. Islam is *not* compatible with American values.

Note: You realize that *generalizations* are broad, and not true in *every* case, you know that right? Few of us are so arrogant to think that some general statement, such as the above regarding Muslims, is true in *all* cases, that should be obvious. But, generalizations are *generally* true. I'm not talking about the Muslims who live next door to you, necessarily, or those you work with, or go to school with, or even *you* if you're a Muslim. I'm talking about

Muslims as a *global* entity, and Islam as it is understood in the hearts and minds of the majority of devout Muslims worldwide. If you've read polls that surveyed Muslims about their approval of violent tactics, including approval of the attacks of 9-11, or limiting women's rights, or on homosexuality, or their view on Islam and world domination, you'll see that Islam is a *radical* and *violent* religion, quite set apart from the world's other religions. Although this view in some circles is automatically viewed as "hate speech" or some vile lie, this is actually *not* some anti-Muslim rhetoric, it's a reflection on the *facts* surrounding Islam and the opinions of Muslims around the world. Again, your goal should be *independent* research into controversial subjects, not taking the word of either side of a topic on face value. People will lie to you, and people will distort the truth, often under the guise of *political correctness* which seeks to suppress such facts. Set emotion aside, and discover the *facts*, then you'll be prepared to form an opinion.

When trying to pick sides on the issues mentioned or deciding who to believe when you hear conflicting "facts," you might want to use your *common sense*. Most of us do have a 'sense' for what is right and wrong, and good and evil. Trust that inner sense and allow common sense to alert you to the obvious.

Let's revisit and add a few thoughts about some of the previous topics.

Abortion. The *pro-choice* movement says it's the woman's body and her choice to keep or kill the baby. But, there's somebody else involved here, and it's the *baby*. She *chose* to get pregnant. We know how to prevent pregnancy, it's simple, and it's inexpensive; she *chose* to get pregnant, perhaps through negligence, but she *chose* to be negligent, and now a life has been created. The pro-**choice** argument is "That's her business." Liberals tell us that killing the baby is no big deal, nothing to be concerned with, and none of anyone else's business.

The *pro-life* movement reminds us that it's a *baby*, a human life, and that we should be very careful about allowing the indiscriminate killing of babies. The pro-life view would have the woman choose adoption if she doesn't want the baby, not death. Very early on the baby looks and acts like a baby. The baby has a heartbeat, it moves around, it kicks its feet, it sucks it thumb, it can feel pain. An abortion often involves the ripping apart of the baby, limb by limb, after sucking it's brain out and crushing its skull. An abortion is a gruesome procedure. It's not a "thing" it's a *baby*. Which side of this issue are you on and why? Do you know anything about *Margaret Sanger*, the founder of *Planned Parenthood?* You should read about her, she was a racist, whose main intention was the killing of *black* babies. You must have known that, especially if you support pro-choice and the *Planned Parenthood* organization, right? Can you guess which population of people has the most abortions, most often with the support and encouragement of Planned Parenthood? Yes, it's mostly black people killing *black* babies, by a huge margin. At some point you might discover you have been played by liberals, and that their indoctrination has a goal, this abortion agenda is just one example.

Guns. School shootings are *rare*, but they trigger a visceral and highly *emotional* response. Liberals easily push aside facts in favor of emotion, and emotion is easily exploited to further a political agenda. The liberal agenda, is to get rid of all guns in civilian hands, coming door to door to take them away if you don't give them up. I imagine they'd delete that Second Amendment first, but that's the goal. They'll tell you no, that's not the plan, and they just want "common sense gun control." But, they want to start small and go big, their plan is to take guns away, since you don't *need* them. They might let you own a gun, if you keep in locked up at the shooting range and go there to use it to shoot targets. They actually propose such things. They seem to forget that our founders weren't much interested in you shooting at targets or hunting for deer, they were concerned with the ability of citizens to protect themselves from the GOVERNMENT. You know the difference between automatic and semi-automatic weapons? And I imagine you know the difference between an "assault rifle" and a *regular* rifle? Most liberals have VERY limited knowledge about guns, yet support laws to deal with them, not even understanding what differentiates one from the other.

About **10 children <u>per year</u> have been killed in school shootings** during a 30-year study. *Eleven* young people die **per <u>DAY</u>** from accidents involving texting and driving, that's over **4000 young people per year, dead because of texting** and driving. If it's all about saving the lives of our children, I guess we need to take those phones away? Cows kill 20 people per year, dogs kill 28, and bees, wasps, and hornets kill 58. Deaths from school shootings are *rare*. A minimum of 67,000 crimes, including rape, murder, and assaults are ***prevented*** each year by the use of a gun in the hands of an innocent law-abiding citizen. The statistics can vary wildly, depending on the source, but one thing is clear, the United States has millions of guns, our Constitution made gun ownership the second of our amendments, and getting rid of guns in the U.S. is *quite* unlikely in any foreseeable future. Even if all guns were taken away from law-abiding citizens, *millions* would still exist in the hands of **criminals**. Just a little common sense will allow you to conclude we won't be getting rid of guns, and it isn't even a good idea. The main reason for the regular call for more and more gun restrictions is prompted by the extremely rare Spector of school shootings. We already have strict background checks, it's NOT easy to buy a gun, and the guns used in school shootings are usually legally obtained guns. I'll agree that parents not keeping their guns locked up and out of the hands of their children is a real problem, and is one law that would make sense, especially if those parents of school shooters were *harshly* prosecuted for allowing their child to get that gun.

One recurring idea is to allow *teachers* who want to carry a gun to do so. Liberals tend to think that idea is CRAZY. Would a shooter be likely to enter a school intent on killing people if they knew they would be facing perhaps dozens of armed teachers? Common sense will say no, they'd probably go elsewhere to do their shooting. That little common-sense test above also gives you some important insight. We could allow teachers to arm themselves tomorrow, and that move would most likely save lives, immediately, but we don't do that, we *talk* instead, and come up with expensive and complicated plans. Is it really about saving lives? Or, is it some political agenda about getting rid of guns? If we were to spend millions and millions of dollars to harden our schools, (which is probably the "solution" our politicians and liberals will choose) with the addition of fences, metal detectors, armed guards, etc., the next school shooter would simply become the *school parking lot shooter*, or the *grad night party shooter*, or the *shooting the crowd waiting to go through the metal detector shooter*, taking their murderous plans to whatever easier target they can find, and they *would* find it. If no guns are available, killers chose knives, or cars, or whatever. The answer is in the *brains* of those young people who choose to kill, and in discovering what is negatively impacting them. Could video games all about killing people be a factor? Could a society of permissive parents be to blame? How about a lack of firm discipline at home and school? All those things will be pushed aside as we focus on *guns*. It isn't only our youth who don't initiate enough critical thinking, we have lots of beauacrats with the same problem.

When you rely on common sense and facts, in place of emotion, you see much more clearly. Can you do that, can you use common sense and facts, or will the emotional side of such issues blind you to those facts? While reading this little book, you should be getting a sense of what sort of person you are, prone to emotion, or prone towards facts and common sense. If you don't like what you've discovered, you can change.

Global warming. This is closely tied to oil, since the global warming "science" is all about carbon dioxide in the atmosphere causing the earth to heat up as burning petroleum releases CO2. The problem is, it probably doesn't do that, man-made CO2 probably doesn't heat the earth, at least not much. And, according to the *United Nations* study that is relied on by liberals, even if the United States stopped ALL of its carbon emissions, it would take *hundreds of years* to see a change. Of course the U.S. can't come close to stopping *all* carbon emissions, and the worst offenders around the world would not join us since their emerging economies rely on oil as energy, so, we can't do anything about it, according to the U.N's own report. Anything we do to cut our CO2 emissions will have almost no effect on this supposed problem, and not for hundreds of years. There's also a little common sense to be applied here, what is the earth's perfect temperature? Is it the temperature we've been used to in our lifetimes? The lifetimes of our grandparents? We do know that areas now covered in snow were once topical, and desert areas were once covered in glaciers; long before the arrival of man and his CO2. The earth's climate and temperature changes, it has cycles, largely attributed to the cycles of the sun and to changing ocean currents.

So why all this global warming hysteria? The U.S. would be the main participant in proposed global warming plans, distributing our wealth to other nations on earth though fines, and our economy would be slowed dramatically, affecting all our standards of living, for a goal that is clearly unobtainable. It's about power, control, economics, and a move to make the U.S. less influential, and less powerful in the world. Does that sound like a good plan? If you say yes, you might need to rethink the pros and cons.

Borders. If you take away hatred of brown people as a reason, and look at the facts, the facts are clear. First, hatred of brown people is a manufactured liberal lie, wanting a strong border is the norm, all countries have borders. We would still need a strong border and strong immigration rules if Mexico's population all looked like blonde blue-eyed Swedes, it's not about being brown or Mexican, it's about being a net plus to our economy and not a burden. Crime IS a problem with Mexican illegal immigrants, they commit thousands and thousands of violent and other crimes every year, including many rapes and murders. *Mexico's* immigration laws are strict, much stronger than U.S. laws. You can't just walk into Mexico and get free school, free medical care, welfare, and start protesting that Mexico needs to treat you like a citizen, you'll end up quickly deported or in a Mexican prison. A strong border is simply a common sense obvious reality. We want *legal* immigrants who want to assimilate and become *Americans*, and we want people who are educated, will become self-reliant, and hopefully have some skill that we need. A country needs firm control of immigration, and borders that actually keep those out who don't belong. It's not that crazy is it?

P.S. There are many many millions of people in shithole countries (was that too descriptive?) who would like to come to the U.S., but we simply can't afford to accept massive numbers of the world's poor and unskilled. Other countries, virtually ALL other countries, are VERY picky about who can live in their countries, because they are putting *their citizens* first. But we do have a cautionary tale, to help us visualize the impact of large-scale indiscriminate immigration, we can see the results of open immigration; when France, Germany, England, and other countries jumped on the largely Muslim immigration bandwagon, they soon realized what happens with such massive open immigration. Those countries are in the throes of losing their cultural identities, as Muslims attempt to bring *their* country and culture into replace the endemic culture, with no intention of assimilation. Crime, violence, and sexual assault on women and children, by mostly Muslim immigrants, has skyrocketed in all those countries. The economic well-being and the safety of *our citizens* SHOULD be our first priority, not opening up the U.S. to all who would like to come. Common sense?

~

I could go on and on, but you get the picture. There are other sides to every issue. You should seek to recognize areas where *emotion* is pushing aside facts and be careful. Such plays on emotion are often a ploy to push some *agenda*. Often those agendas are exposed when you know the facts. *Critical thinking* is about searching out facts in the tangle of emotion and political agendas. Much, perhaps *most*, of politics is about *power and control*, and many of these issues we've been discussing here put vast power into the hands of a few select politicians.

Too many of us are too easily played, *they* know this, and they use this. The liberal professor who berates and degrades the student with an opposing view is a window into this manipulation. It is commonplace for the conservative speaker on a liberal campus, if invited at all, to be shouted down, to encounter violent protests, and to have their views shut down by the other side, who label their speech *hateful*, and seek to disallow it. It's becoming difficult to even *hear* the opposing viewpoint on the college campus, let alone civilly debate it.

It is common for someone wearing a *"Make America Great Again"* hat to be yelled and cursed at, and to be the target of violence and intimidation. That's the left, that's the liberal play book. You won't find stories about liberals wearing a Hillary shirt being violently accosted, but you'll find many many such reports about conservatives wearing a Trump shirt or hat. Those acts are regular occurrences, even now, long *after* the election.

Trump. Liberals have lost their minds when it comes to Donald Trump. Hillary was *supposed* to win, and the liberal world has been turned on its axis with the Trump Presidency. The "news" about Trump IS slanted and now obviously and openly so. Liberal *journalism* **has** become "fake news."

Hillary Clinton was a terrible candidate. Barack Obama was a terrible President. You might think I've ventured into *my* view and away from facts, but I haven't. By any measure Barack Obama was a failed President.

Again, competing phonebooks full of opposing information and opinions could be presented here, but a fair review of the facts will demonstrate this to be true. One example, *The Iran Deal*. President Obama couldn't get congress to agree to such a "deal" which could have become an enforceable and binding *treaty* with their support, so he simply made an *agreement* with Iran. The short version, we gave them TONS of money (literally, delivered in huge cargo planes in cash) and they promised to *slow down* their nuclear bomb development, for a few years. Ultimately the agreement *allows* Iran to have nuclear weapons, a clear departure from the past policy of never allowing Iran, or other dangerous dictatorships and terrorist nations to have nuclear weapons. This was a terrible, costly, dangerous, and stupid deal. President Trump quickly reversed this deal and is returning to a policy of non-proliferation of nuclear weapons, especially in the hands of such dangerous countries. Common sense says good for Trump. Obama's healthcare plan is another example. One after another the healthcare providers bailed out of the Obamacare plan, which was costing them a fortune and not delivering better care. People lost the doctors and medical plans that Obama had promised they could keep, and the cost of health insurance skyrocketed. In case you don't know, socialist healthcare plans in other countries are not FREE, nothing is free, taxes are raised to pay for "free" things. American health care is the envy of most other countries, it's not uncommon to wait many months for tests and procedures under such socialized medical systems. During the Obama years the liberals would talk of people dying in the streets because they didn't have health insurance. It was then, and has been for many decades, a requirement that hospitals *must* treat life-threatening illnesses and injuries, regardless of your ability to pay. You knew that right? Well it's true, nobody was dying in the street because they didn't have health insurance and the hospital refused to treat their life-threatening illness or injury, that was a lie, with a purpose behind it, you were being played, to support their socialist healthcare changes. President Trump is in the process of salvaging the wreckage Obama created, and the free market and *choice* will be the key, not some plan mandated by a political party.

Race. This was perhaps Barack Obama's biggest opportunity, and his biggest failure. The Obama years were punctuated by constant divisions based on color. He was quick to call out and blame the police in police shooting or abuse cases before the facts were known. He sowed the seeds of a new and energized war on the police based on race. None of the most publicized police shooting cases found the police at fault. Did you know that? You'd think these shootings of black men by predominantly white police officers were all cases of murderous racism, but they weren't. The victims weren't innocent, and the vast majority of such incidents were found to be justified, even by Obama's Justice Department headed by a black Attorney General. Instead of bringing us together as one people and moving away from the emphasis on our colors, he encouraged it, he tossed logs on the fire dividing us by color more than ever.

The problems experienced by many black people are the problems brought to them by the democrats controlling the cities they live in. The war on poverty and the increasing dependence on welfare has destroyed the black family. Single mothers, unemployment, poor education, abortion, drug use, all results of largely liberal policies.

A year into the Trump Presidency and black unemployment is at an *all time* low. Liberal policies have been hurting black people for decades. Conservative polices under President Trump are ushering in a boom in manufacturing, employment, and prosperity. The full effect is yet to be realized, but black communities are already feeling the positive effects. Was that commentary or fact? Watching the liberal media, one might have a whole different set of "facts." Somebody is telling the truth, and somebody is lying to you.

~

If my premise at the beginning of this book was correct, many of you reading this have a *whole* different take on everything I've said. You might believe that this was simply one lie after another from a racist, gun-loving, Trump supporter. If so, you've proven my point.

"This liberal indoctrination/*brainwashing* is present in the majority of social media, the *news*, in Hollywood movies and television shows, comedy, etc., in just about every aspect of life young people will face a constant onslaught of the *liberal* view of things, the liberal viewpoint is the predominant viewpoint in schools, and in most "mainstream" media."

That was early on in this little book, but too true. You have a choice, you can ignore this book, and dismiss it as hateful conservative propaganda, or you can accept the fact that you haven't done much critical thinking on these topics, that you have allowed yourself to be manipulated, indeed brainwashed, and now you can do something about it.

~

I teach a college course. It's an EMT (Emergency Medical Technician) course, so politics isn't a highlight of that class, but *critical thinking* is. I'm going to use this book in my EMT course. The EMT needs to have lots of *common sense*, and to make quick decisions based not only on their training but on that good common sense and judgment.

We should all try to be *thinkers*. We should all strive to *lead* rather than follow, and to think *independently*. If we get our "news" from the liberal social media, it *will* have a liberal bias. Sadly, the liberal bias is much more likely to suppress facts, and appeal to emotion in an attempt to control your thinking.

Conservative media is also biased, but more likely to offer up a more factual pro and con. Generally, don't trust *any* one source, seek out facts where you can, pay special attention to any 'news' source that seems based primarily on the *emotional* argument, and treat it as a red flag, and make up your own mind. If you hate Donald Trump, you should be able to articulate *why*. If your "reasons" seem to center on emotion not fact, you should rethink and research.

I can't stand Barack Obama, not because he's black, I don't care what color he is, I could vote for a black man or woman for President, if they had good conservative values I agreed with. But not Obama; he wanted to "transform" this country into something other than the America we know, he was too loose on immigration and too appeasing to Muslim enemies. He had a contempt for our Constitution, he saw America as too powerful and too influential and wanted to distribute American wealth around the world to the detriment of American citizens. He saw the world as racially divided, not embracing that dream of Martin Luther King but stalling it. He told us to accept the new normal of America in decline, in manufacturing, and as a world power. He was weak on our border, weak on economic development, and weak on the world stage. He sought to dismantle our coal industry and to slow down our oil production. He said fuel costs would "necessarily skyrocket" as he cut back on coal and oil. He was willing to drastically slow our economy in pursuit of his misguided view of global warming. He called republican Presidents unpatriotic for our large national debt but increased it *massively* under his watch. He put restraints on our military through Washington micro-management, costing lives and making the job harder for our warriors. Just to name a few things that immediately come to mind, and there's much more. Bengasi, the IRS scandal, the *Fast and Furious* scandal, and the soon to be uncovered illegal spying and interference with the Trump campaign by his FBI, CIA, and DOJ. So, I can't stand Barack Obama, but I have some reasons, and none of them have to do with his skin color.

Now it's up to you. In my EMT class we'll have a brief discussion about this book and what's in it. I'll ask my students who disagree with something I've said to support their argument. We'll see if they can support their views with facts, or if it's all about feelings and emotion. It's an EMT class, so we won't spend much time on politics, but *critical thinking* is important! Students should be treated as the *whole student*, where even a math class might become an opportunity to encourage and nurture critical thinking! The students in my class, like all students, will go out into the world, they are voters, they will shape the future, they will lead it, and I hope they are *independent thinkers*, not lemmings following some party or agenda or person blindly.

A discussion of critical thinking is best illustrated with controversial topics, hence this book and these topics. Critical thinking is something you'll need to do every day, especially when it comes to the important topics that influence your life. This book, and this subject, is important, and I hope these discussions have opened your eyes to a broader way of thinking about the world around you.

An *epiphany* is a sudden enlightenment, a door opening to a new way of looking at things, like a light bulb lighting up. Perhaps some of you have had such an epiphany and can now see things in a different way, perhaps more clearly. I hope so.

I hope I can encourage such thinking, so that the next time some political topic pops up on your social media you might not be so quick to "Like" it, not until you *understand* it.

Lance Hodge

"An education isn't how much you have committed to memory, or even how much you know. It's being able to differentiate between what you do know and what you don't."

- Anatole France

"It is the mark of an educated mind
to be able to entertain a thought
without accepting it."

- Aristotle

"If you think education is expensive,
try ignorance."

- Derek Bok

"It is today we must create the
world of the future."

- Eleanor Roosevelt

"It is the supreme art of the teacher
to awaken joy in creative expression
and knowledge."

- Albert Einstein

"The objective of education is to prepare the young to educate themselves throughout their lives."

- Robert Maynard Hutchins

"Do not go where the path may lead; go instead where there is no path and leave a trail."

- Ralph Waldo Emerson

"Education would be much more effective if its purpose was to ensure that by the time they leave school every boy and girl should know how much they do not know, and be imbued with a lifelong desire to know it."

- William Haley, British Editor

"Too often we give children answers
to remember rather than problems
to solve."

- Roger Lewin

"The eye sees only what the mind is
prepared to comprehend."

- Henri Bergson, French Philosopher and Educator

"If you think you can, you can. And
if you think you can't, you're right."

- MARY KAY ASH, American businesswoman

"Children are not vessels to be filled
but lamps to be lit."

- SWAMI CHINMAYANANDA,
Indian Spiritual Leader

"Mistakes are a fact of life. It is the response to the error that counts."

- NIKKI GIOVANNI, American poet

"The one real goal of education is to leave a person asking questions."

- MAX BEERHOHM, British Critic, Essayist, and Caricaturist

"He who asks a question is a fool for five minutes; he who does not ask a question remains a fool forever."

- CHINESE PROVERB

"No problem can be solved by the same consciousness that created it. We need to see the world anew."

- ALBERT EINSTEIN

"The important thing is not to stop questioning."

- Albert Einstein

"Knowing a great deal is not the same as being smart; intelligence is not information alone but also judgment, the manner in which information is collected and used."

- Carl Sagan

"There is nothing more uncommon than common sense."

- FRANK LLOYD WRIGHT

"Time given to thought is the greatest time saver of all."

- Norman Cousins

"Think for yourselves and let others
enjoy the privilege to do so, too"

- Voltaire

"Reason obeys itself: ignorance
submits to what is dictated to it."

- Thomas Paine